Inspiration

A Gift of Poems, Insights and Affirmations

ARPress
45 Dan Road Suite 36
Canton MA 02021

Hotline: 1(888) 821-0229
Fax: 1(508) 545-7580

Ordering Information:
Quantity Sales. Special discounts are available on quantity purchases by corporations, associations, and others. For details, contact the publisher at the address above.

Printed in the United States of America.

ISBN-13   Paperback   979-8-89389-628-2
                 Hardcover   979-8-89389-629-9
                 eBook   979-8-89389-630-5

Library of Congress Control Number: 2024921308

Inspiration

A Gift of Poems, Insights and Affirmations

CARRIE BELL HARRELL-WINNS

ACKNOWLEDGEMENT

Honoring "Mother White" RosaLee Canteen White, age 102, soon to be 103, November 7, 2018.
To God be the glory

Without you both, Ms. Stacy Adams and Ms. Hannah Lopez,
my original book would be lifeless. Thank you for bringing my book to life.

DEDICATION

In loving memories of

The late Rev. Thomas S. Lance &
The late Sis. Florine Canteen Lance
The late Major J. Miller
"Uncle D"

The late Sgt. Donald Lee Rice
"Anyway it goes, I will be alright."

The late Dec. Raymond Lance
"Uncle Friday"

The late E. John Holmes

Mother Rosalee Canteen White

THE SPIRIT OF THE LORD

The Spirit of the Lord is…
Love
Peace
Joy
Long-suffering
Kindness
Goodness
Faithfulness
Gentleness
Giving
Self-Control

The Spirit of the Lord, is a gift from God.

THE SPIRIT OF MY LORD

The Spirit of My Lord is Love.
The Spirit of My Lord is Peace.
The Spirit of My Lord is Joy.
The Spirit of My Lord is Giving.
The Spirit of My Lord is Forgiving.
The Spirit of My Lord is a Gift.
This Gift comes from God.

INNER GUIDANCE

Yes! There is a spirit within.
It's not hard to find.
Just focus on the Almighty
Oh! He can be so kind.

Once I was a retch undone;
Full of sin, you know the one.
Then one day I met the Master
An inspiration, and full of laughter.
He said, my child, I have a gift for you.
This is what you must do.
Seek Me first, and never doubt,
I will be there; you don't have to shout.

INNER GUIDANCE

The gift of inner guidance
Is a pure as cotton.
Once you've found it,
It will not be forgotten.

Like a descending dove,
It is as simple as love.

It shoots like a dart.
It's in your heart.

INNER BEAUTY

Inner beauty fills my soul.
Inner beauty will never grow old.

A delicate red rose will last several days,
But inner beauty will never fade away.

This inner beauty has existed within me;
Ten, twenty, thirty, forty, now fifty-three.

Words can never speak so well,
The inner beauty I held.

A gift O' Lord have you given me.
For when I die, I will bring it back to Thee.

NOT DEPRESSED

I

Am Not

Depressed.

I

Am BLESSED.

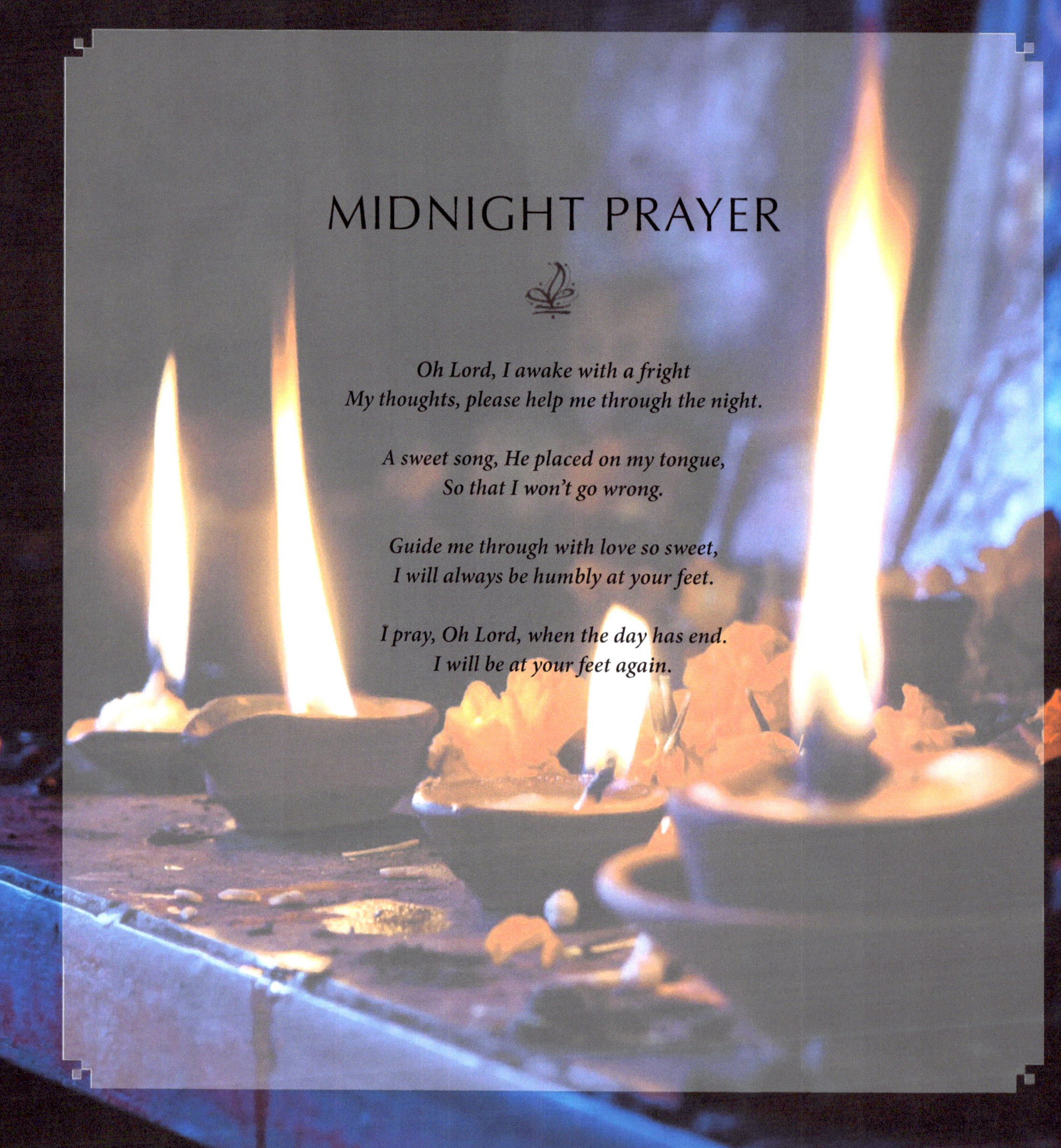

MIDNIGHT PRAYER

Oh Lord, I awake with a fright
My thoughts, please help me through the night.

A sweet song, He placed on my tongue,
So that I won't go wrong.

Guide me through with love so sweet,
I will always be humbly at your feet.

I pray, Oh Lord, when the day has end.
I will be at your feet again.

DARK DAYS

Dark days can be brighten
Fear not, don't be frighten.

Depression is like a prison,
Focus on God, and be risen.

Dark Mondays can be blue,
But God's love is forever true.

When you feel yourself going astray,
Just kneel down and pray.
Say! Lord, help me go the extra mile
Oh! He'll let you face it with a smile.

When the prayer is done,
No! Don't run.
You thank God,
Then go have fun.

Dark days has come and gone.
But, the love of God continues on.

HIDDEN MAN

There is a hidden man in your heart.
Keep in touch with Him, He will never depart.

He monitors every word you say.
Something He does day by day.

He is the King
He makes your heart sing

He is a Spirit, you see,
So! Let Him be.

Let him have His way.
His promise to you, you won't go astray.

Put your trust in the hidden man,
He is the only one that can;
Lift you up when you are down,
He'll place your feet on solid ground.

When you feel you have nothing to gain.
The hidden man tells you, come out of the rain.

When you thought you were dying,
The rain was drying.

The Hidden man said,
You are flying.

GRAY DAYS

Yesterday was so gray.
Lord, I thank you for this day.
That day has past and gone.
My prayer, Oh Lord, help me to go on.

In the stillness of my soul,
Your words abide, and never grow old.

I feel your presence all around,
My Spirit tells me, You won't let me down.
Sometimes Satan tries to attack,
My Spirit tells Satan step back.

Satan is a dirty crook;
To defeat him, read "The Book".

Today is another day.
Lord, I thank you it's not gray.

FORGIVENESS

Oh Lord I rejoice not when my enemies fall;
Instead my prayer is they stand tall.

Forgiveness is like a cloud swept away.
It is not like a mountain of clay.

A forgiving Lord is the one I know.
He is my Master with the glow.

O Lord I hearken to your voice.
I know you'll give me an eternal choice.

Oh Lord thank you for a forgiven Spirit,
I know you are buried deep within it.

Oh Lord my prayer for my enemies and my foes.
I know my reward is a crown of gold.

PEACEMAKER

Peacemaker is a counselor of joy.
Oh! No, no, no, He's not a toy.

Search your soul and avoid strife,
For strife can cut just like a knife.

Live life from day to day,
With only good words to say.

Have peace within your heart,
Because that is where it starts.

To be a peacemaker is an honor,
You will find love around every corner.

Trust in God, and do your best.
True peacemaker, God will do the rest.

SPIRITUAL AFFIRMATION

I thank God for the "Gift of the Holy Spirit"
I have spiritual wisdom; it is the key to the Kingdom.
I am renewed in my Spirit every second.
I have a divine Spirit that surrounds me.
I am calm and collected by my inner Spirit.
It's okay for me to have fun and still love the Lord.
The gift of God fills my life with abundance.
God's light is a gift that attracts.
I have peace with the inner man.
I always forgive and start new.
I have peace and serenity daily.
I have a deep root of divine order.
I always prosper with the love of God.

SPIRITUAL AFFIRMATION

(continued)

The more I love God, the more I love myself.
The more I love myself, the more I love my fellow man.
I am a beaming light.
I help lift God with my little light.
My life is filled with the beauty of God's love.
I love God, and I am free.
I am not bound, I am free.
I am filled with His blessings.
God gave me power to master my life.
Deep within me, I am so strong.
My heart is filled with love.
I love what God has made me.
My feelings are a part of me and I accept myself.

SPIRITUAL AFFIRMATION
(continued)

I love the word LOVE, and I love being loved.
Freely, I give my love to others.
I can do all thing through God's invested power.
I am now wealthy with His perfect peace.
I have a one-on-one relationship with God.
I don't have a job and I am richly blessed.
I am thankful God placed ne where He wants me to be.
I am guided by "The Spirit", God's Spirit guides me.
I have everything I need.
I have obtained God's riches (LOVE).
I accept the riches of God's abundant blessings.
Every day, I am basking in His infinite riches.

SPIRITUAL AFFIRMATIONS

(continued)

I turn negatives into positives daily.
I am going to give freely, and look for nothing in return.
I enjoy the things I do because God is in the plan.
I am happy to be a part of "God's Master Plan".
I thank God I am able to move and think.
I am grateful to God for the miracles in my life.
I exercise my mind daily with positive thinking.
My heart is a strong place for love.
I read "The Word" daily, it strengthens me.
God gave me a key; I am able to unlock my own spiritual treasurers.
I have a healthy heart; I think positive thoughts.
I affirm my daily affirmations.
I have a positive mental attitude in Christ Jesus.

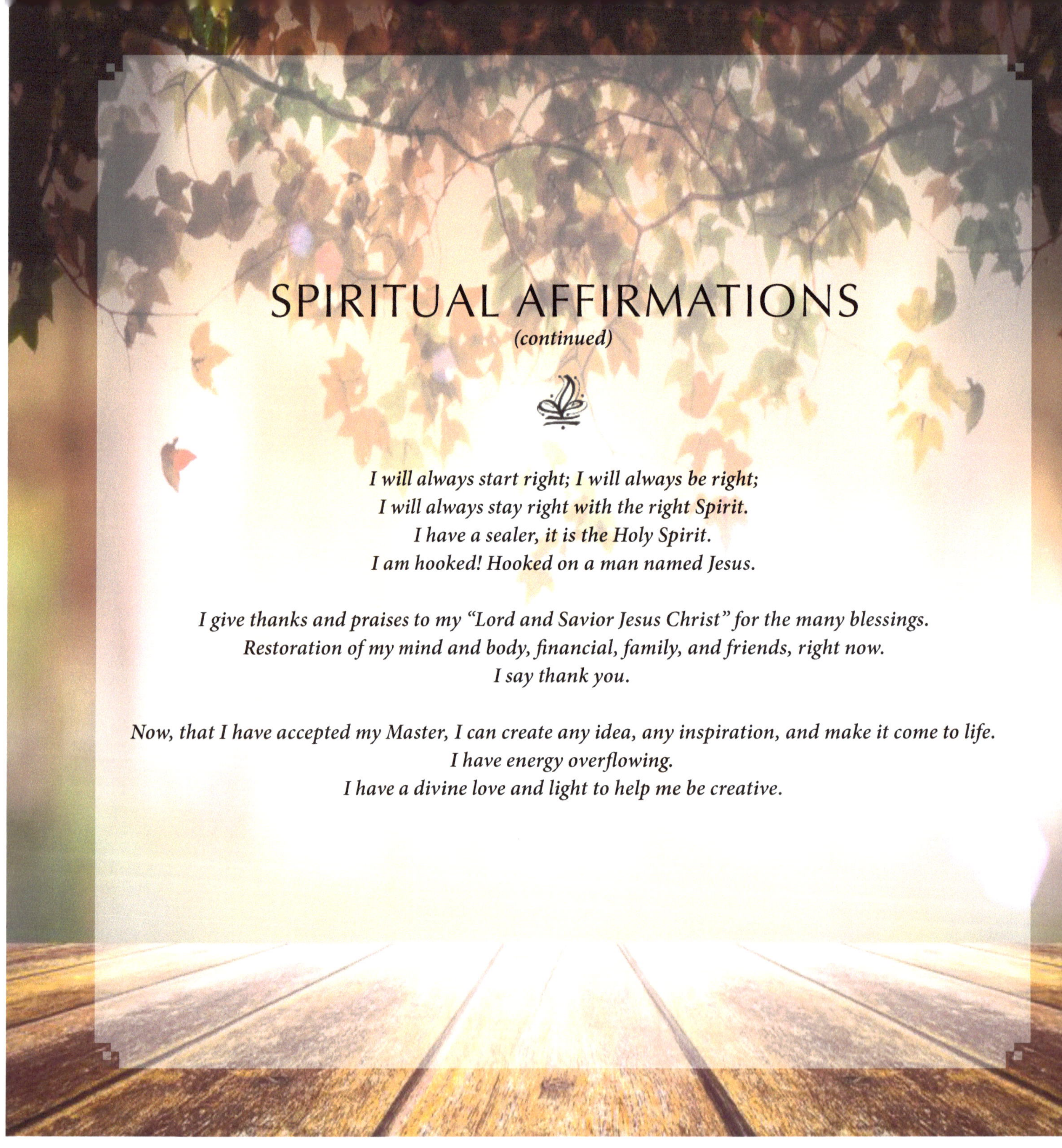

SPIRITUAL AFFIRMATIONS

(continued)

I will always start right; I will always be right;
I will always stay right with the right Spirit.
I have a sealer, it is the Holy Spirit.
I am hooked! Hooked on a man named Jesus.

I give thanks and praises to my "Lord and Savior Jesus Christ" for the many blessings.
Restoration of my mind and body, financial, family, and friends, right now.
I say thank you.

Now, that I have accepted my Master, I can create any idea, any inspiration, and make it come to life.
I have energy overflowing.
I have a divine love and light to help me be creative.

SPIRITUAL AFFIRMATIONS

(continued)

I accept my Lord and Savior.
I thank the Almighty for making me a part of His "Master Plan" today.
I give God thanks for my health, wealth, happiness, and a peace of mind.
Knowing, where it all started,
"Calvary" I thank God, that where I am, He is there.
I love you Lord.
Amen.

COMFORT

In the coolness of the day,
All my tears forever whipped away.
Gladness and joy overcome sorrow,
Then I knew there was hope for tomorrow.

Oh! How I welcome death with a smile,
I don't mind entertaining it for a while.
My comforting Savior waits for me, Satan,
please just let me be.

I'll wait here in God's cool shade
I seek comfort under the tree He made.
The divine comforter is coming you see,
I'll continue to wait here under His tree.

SKY

Look at the sky from one end to the other,
Thanks to you, does it go any further.

Look in amazement from side-to-side,
There's really no place to hide.

Even in the dark clouds so thick,
There's no hiding there it's only a trick.

Trust in your heart with all your might,
The dark clouds are not like the night.

Look at the sky with all its miles,
Just thank God and smile.

LIFE

When I was born, God gave me a brain.
I travel through this world with a lot to gain.

During my youth, I ventured from the main,
Now, I am old and body racking with pain.

As a young adult I remained plain,
Not knowing when to come out of the rain.

Now, I am older, I need a trip to Spain,
Now, I am so old, Lord, I'll just wait on your train.

LISTEN

Listen to the words and hear,
Do not doubt nor fear.
The Lord gives the words to be used,
Only we have the mind to choose.

The Holy Spirit is the key,
It is hidden deep in your heart you see.
It is delightful and such a charm,
Use it wisely, it will not harm.

Then you'll know that you're blessed,
Because you'll no longer be distressed.
Count your blessings and be glad,
Oh! That was not so bad.

So why should you dwell,
In the pits of Satan's hell.
For God gave His only Son, that we might live,
In the Mansion that Hi gives.

BROKEN HEART

Jesus died on the cross for our sins.
The Blood and the water came from his heart.
The weight of all our sins Killed our
Lord and Savior
How can we repay our Lord, Jesus?
LOVE

GONE, BUT NOT FORGOTTEN

"A tree stands tall and strong
As the man who planted it"
This tree is dedicated to "MJM"
In loving Memory,
The Red-Tip-Tree Blooms in
April
Feeling empty and blessed
all at the same time.
This is a testament to all those missing a love one today.
But know this:
There resting in the arms of the All Mighty.
Gone, but not forgotten.

Amen, Amen, Amen.

REINCARNATION
OF INSPIRATION
MY ANGEL
MsCarrieBell

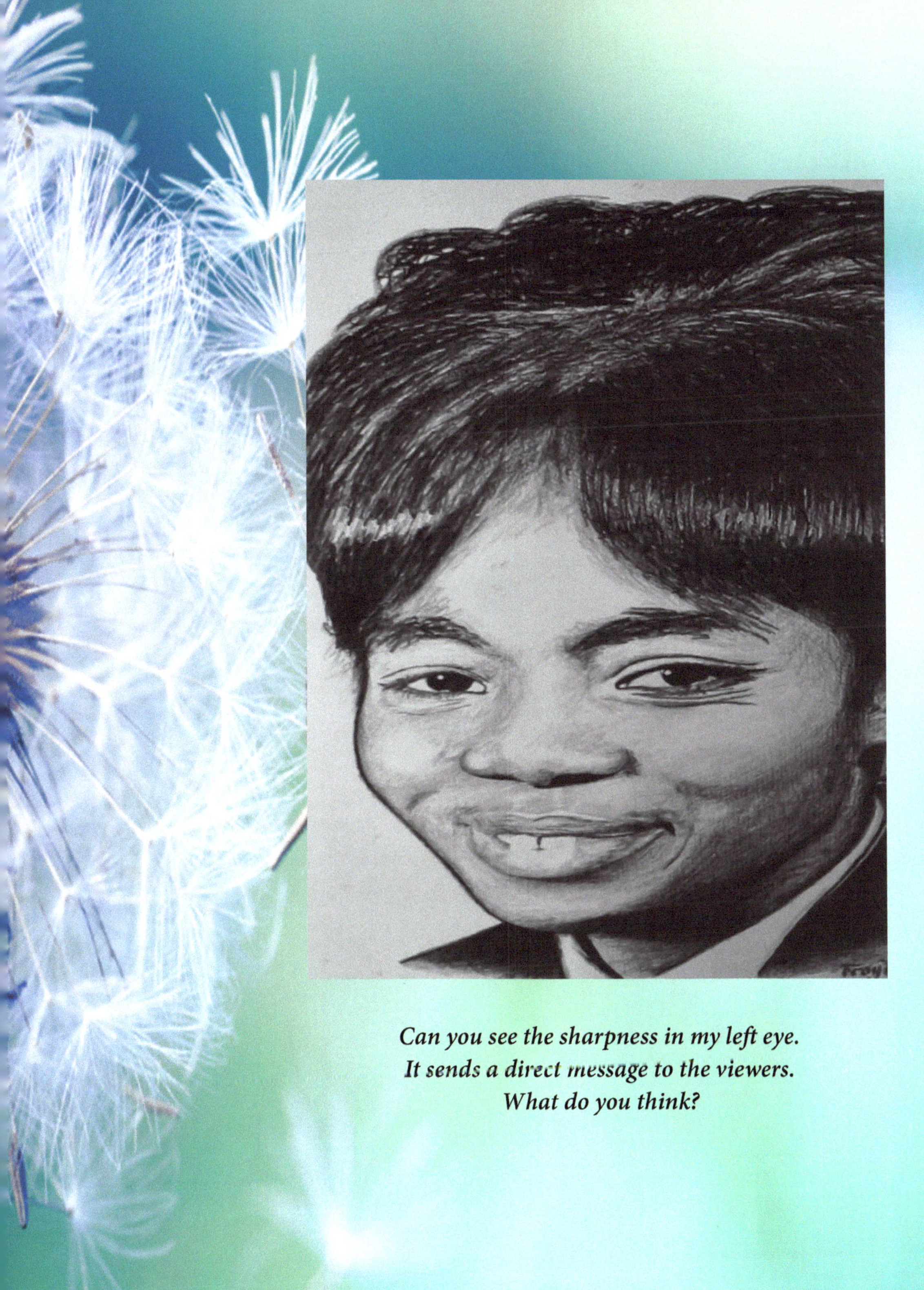

Can you see the sharpness in my left eye.
It sends a direct message to the viewers.
What do you think?